1

Table of Contents

INTRODUCTION

While most people spend the majority of their time indoors, most of us are still undeniably drawn outside to soak in the sights and sounds of nature. There's just something about the sunshine, green grass, pretty flowers, sweet fragrances, and animals that make the outdoors relaxing and rejuvenating.

Do you have a nice outdoor space to retreat to at your home or business? If not, it's something worth consideration. In fact, a beautifully landscaped lawn can make a world of difference for your family or customers. It will boost curb appeal, improve a first impression, and generate positive feelings. Whether you're looking to add some greenery, flower beds, bubbling water features, or other enhancements to your yard or commercial property, consider the range of benefits you can expect from adding diverse landscaping to your property.

Landscape Design:

1. Determine Landscape Needs and Wants

Make a list of needs and wants. do your kids need a play space, do you want to grow vegetables, would your family gather on a patio Do some very rough sketches of the yard with thoughts of where you want to place things; it's a great organizing principle for landscape design for beginners. They don't need to be master plans (they can just be ideas).

2. Think About Location

Study the sun and wind patterns. You might want to place a patio on the west side of the house, but it will get lots of afternoon sun, which means dinnertime in August won't be relaxing just hot. And wind whistling around a corner will quickly extinguish a fire pit. Those are common mistakes in backyard landscape design for beginners. Your design should take into account what the sun and wind do at different times of the day and year.

3. Sit Down and Enjoy Your Landscape

Live with it for a while. Coming to ⬚uick conclusions about your yard can lead to choices that don't work in the long term. After spending more time outdoors, you'll start to see areas where you want to go and sit that you wouldn't have thought of at first, Lipanovich says.

4. Start Small

Home and garden television shows are masters at revealing complete outdoor makeovers in just three days but they have a crew of 60, which is not a situation enjoyed by most beginner gardeners. Part of creating a landscape is slowly developing a plan and enjoying the process. From your master plan, start with a small flower bed. Go out and work on it for an hour or two when you have the time, and worry less about filling everything up right away. Take your time, so you don't take shortcuts or get too sloppy with your landscape design.

5. Find a Focal Point

Any good garden design has a focal point or series of focal points, and it's an easy principle to put in place in landscape design for beginners. That may be a sculpture or a stunning plant, a tree, or a series of shrubs. Let the design draw your eyes around the landscape.

6. Focus on Scale and Pacing

It's the trickiest principle in landscape design for beginners, but scale and pacing give your yard a pulled-together look. There will be variations in size, shape, and color, with tall plants against a building or in the back of a flowerbed, and paths that lead people through the space. It is important to find a good balance between repetition and new elements. Repetition gives a sense of cohesion, but you also don't want it to be monotonous. An occasional new element is better than having all different elements throughout.

7. Be Open to Change

Unless you're strongly devoted to something, be honest about what you like and what may fall out of favor.

Remember: Patience is key to landscape design for beginners. If all of that bare space is too much to look at, and the kids and dogs are tracking in mud, rely on temporary solutions annuals, mulch, fast-growing ground covers to cover an area while you're figuring out what you want. You can rely on annuals and small perennials as you're waiting for larger plants to fill in. You can always move them if you realize they're in the wrong spot later on.

LANDSCAPE DESIGN: IDEAS AND ADVICE FOR BEGINNERS

START WITH A PLAN

If you were to hire a professional landscape designer, one of the first things he/she would do is draw up a plot survey of your property, including your backyard and front yard. This is something you can easily do yourself.

Draw a bird's-eye view of your property, noting the placement of all the man-made features (called hardscape) such as buildings, fences, driveways, stonewalls, etc. Boulders, trees, and large shrubs combine with your hardscape to form the "bones" of your landscape. Using graph paper helps, but you don't have to agonize over exact measurements, a sketch that is roughly in proportion will be fine.

Make sure to include the location of your well, septic system, or any buried utility lines. Orient your lot on the compass and note where your sunny and shady spots are. Once you know what you've already got, you can move on to making a list of what you'd like to have. How do you want your garden to look? Start with a few general goals. For example:

Do you want privacy for a patio area?

Do you want to screen an ugly view?

Is your top priority curb appeal/resale-value or a more private (patio) display?

If you already have flower beds, note the successful plants and fill in the blank spots with the colors, heights, foliage, and bloom time you will need to get the desired look. This will help guide you when you are plant shopping. Be sure to make the most of what you've got already. Don't try to change a dry, rocky spot into a vegetable garden. Instead, use it for a rock garden planted with sedums and hen and chicks, which can thrive in the tough conditions. Use containers to accent difficult areas, too. They're a great way to express your design skills on a small scale and can be changed seasonally, if so desired. Look around your neighborhood. Plants come in all colors, shapes, and sizes. What gardens do you like? Which plant colors, shapes, textures, and sizes speak to you?

CHOOSE YOUR STYLE

Your garden should complement your home's architectural style. Gardening is just like decorating the inside of your house, but instead of fabrics, paint, and furniture, you will be using color, texture, shape, size, and placement of plants to create a mood.

Formal: Straight lines; symmetry; and elegant focal points like statues and fountains, manicured lawns, and pruned hedges define this style. Color is secondary to structure and the mood is refined and serene.

Informal: This style is a balance between the formal and natural styles. It involves lots of curves and colors, lush growth, asymmetry, and natural-shaped trees and shrubs. The mood is comfortable and relaxing.

Natural: This style imitates nature, is low-maintenance, and should blend in with the surroundings, which could be anything from a wildflower meadow to a bog. The mood can reflect untamed chaos or just energetic, natural abundance.

ASSESSING YOUR NEEDS

If you have young children or grandchildren, you'll need areas where they can play. Same for pets. Look to incorporate "bulletproof" plants that can take some abuse, like low-growing sedum or ground phlox, which can both take some trampling.

Think about your entryway. Do you want a welcoming front garden that directs visitors to your door? Use straight lines and hardscaped paths to lead visitors where you want them to go. Don't be discouraged by a small garden space. There are tricks you can use to make small plots seem larger, such as lining up paths, gates, and trees to create sight lines that allow the view to flow from one area into another. Also consider that having many small groupings of different colored flowers can make a space seem cluttered, whereas grouping similar colors and textures together can really open up a small space.

Create your own getaway spot. Use larger shrubs and ornamental grasses to cordon off an area for rest and relaxation, like this secluded bench. Here, you can watch over the garden and enjoy the fruits of your labor.

HARDSCAPE, THEN PLANT

It's tempting to start your design with the plants, but it's best to tend to your hardscape first. Once that's in place, you're ready for the fun part: planting! Start by planting trees or shrubs. Begin from the house and work outward. Remember to plan for the mature size of the trees and shrubs to avoid having to move them later, when they outgrow their space! Deciduous shrubs planted in front of evergreens will change the look seasonally. And don't forget to pick some shrubs for winter interest, too, such as witch hazel or forsythia.

Lay out potential flowerbeds with a hose or rope. A few gentle sweeps look more natural than many sharp curves. Borders are usually planted against a wall, fence, or hedge and are viewed from one side only.

Beds present more of a challenge, since they can be seen from all sides. Wide beds and borders need a hard path or stepping stones to allow you to tend the plants without compacting the soil or trampling anything.

Define the edges where your flower garden meets the lawn. A physical barrier made from metal, vinyl, granite, or brick will help to keep grass from encroaching into the beds. Plants in the foreground can be left to spill over this edging, softening the look.

Layer plants according to height. Repeat drifts of similar plants throughout the garden to give it rhythm. Large blocks of one plant will make the most impact when viewed from a distance rather than the polka dot look of many different plants in one area. To combine plants effectively, take into consideration their size, shape, leaf color and texture, flower color, and visual weight. Loose and open or heavy and dense

Bold-leafed plants like hostas combine well with finely textured ones like astilbe. Blue-green, chartreuse, bronze, burgundy, and silver-leafed plants liven up the garden even when they are not in bloom.

Remember that hot colors appear to advance while cool colors recede into the background. White can separate clashing colors and will brighten up a shady spot.

Beginner Landscape Tips
What Do You Want and What Do You Need?

Are you hoping for a place to play, a quiet place for reading, or a combination of both? It may be that you'd like a spot to grow your favorite vegetables and herbs for cooking. To solve this predicament, make a list of your needs and draw a rough sketch of how you'd like everything to fit together. Use this as a starting point.

Assess Your Yard

Next, assess your yard. How does the wind move through it? What is the path of the sun? Create sitting areas out of the line of prevailing winds or block and direct winds with shrubs and trees. Locate the sunniest spots and evaluate the best places to plant trees. It's ideal to have a place to relax and play that is sheltered from the heat of the day. It's also wonderful to create a space that takes advantage of the sun's warmth on cooler days. In addition, understand how you'll get water from one area of your yard to another. Begin by mapping the angle of the sun and by developing a strategy for watering in order to know how and what to plant.

Live In It

Before digging in, it's helpful to live in a space. Until you sit in a spot and take time in one space or another, you may not know how or if it fits in with your plan. Move a chair around and find a different place to sit each day. Take note of possible focal points and how these places interact with your home and the views from windows. How do existing paths work into the mix? Paths that interface with the surrounding environment affect the users' experience, guiding them not just from one place to another but providing engagement.

Keep it Simple

The simplest answer is usually the best. The final decision doesn't need to be complicated or overdone. Instead, include only the things that matter most. Start small and begin with a framework that allows you to easily move from the inside of your house to a bed of flowers, veggie plot, or patio. The best design solutions are often intuitive. For instance, the path you've made across the lawn, while ignoring an existing walkway, could be a clue to the most compelling composition.

Borrowed Views & Focal Points

Don't forget to incorporate the views beyond your yard. Strategically place trees to frame existing views. Create new views by adding a tree or a group of trees as a focal point. Plant trees that provide shade in summer and offer vibrant colors in fall. Consider flowering trees like dogwoods, buckeyes, or crabapples. Flower gardens and perimeter plantings also make colorful focal points. Grow a row of flowering shrubs like hydrangeas near a patio or deck to enrich and enliven your outdoor experience.

What are the Plants You Love?

A garden isn't a garden without plants. Keep a running list of the plants you'd like to grow. Then circle back to your site assessment to see what's possible. If you're working with part shade, it may preclude you from sun loving plants. Make sure to devise a plan for watering based on the needs to your plants. Determine which tools work best with your plan, considering a Flexogen Super Duty Hose with a Thumb Control Watering Nozzle and a timer.

Embrace Change

Note that nothing stays the same. You may decide a new path is needed or your patio is too small. As you evolve and change, so does your landscape.

Beginner's Guide to Landscaping

Here are   steps to transforming your yard form ordinary to extraordinary.

Size up your plot and Analyze your site: You want to make good use of your space, but that's hard to do if you don't know how much space you have. There are a couple different ways of finding your land measurements. It could be through a land survey from your realtor or title office if you own your home, or a plat map from your county office that maps out your land. A land survey is useful in analyzing your space because it will show any dwellings such as buildings, driveways, fences, etc. on your property; whereas a plat map will show the land before any additions. Either way, both should provide you with dimensions of the property, which is what you need.

Plan a design: Now that you know how much space you have to work with you can plan your design. Check out our landscape designs for inspiration. As you're planning a design keep in mind any slopes, drainage patterns, buildings, driveways, sewer lines, septic tanks and underground power lines. You don't want to plant in locations that will affect surrounding structures. It's important to plant the right tree in the right place so that you not only benefit from the cost savings, but to ensure that you're not spending money down the road for tree removal as a result of death or damage.

Select your trees and shrubs: It's time to have some fun! Are you landscaping to add color? A windbreak? Add some shade? All the above? There are several varieties of trees to choose from but depending on your purpose of landscaping there are numerous factors to keep in mind such as size, location, form and shape

Get in the Dirt: Now that you have your new trees and shrubs it's time to plant. Proper planting and care is crucial, especially for younger seedlings. A common mistake when planting younger seedlings is to use fertilizer or potting soil. Steer away from any commercial soils or fertilizers. Despite their convincing labels, most products contain chemicals and other harmful substances that may cause root burn or kill young seedlings. It's okay to use these products a year or two after planting, when your trees or shrubs are more established, but in their early years they are simply not strong enough to withstand such products. Stick with an all-natural compost or make your own fertilizer.

Maintain your design: Tree maintenance is important, but it doesn't have to be an extensive routine. Water, mulch, and keep an eye out for any unusual changes in your tree.

Cheap Landscaping Ideas for the Backyard
1. Use Mulch Alternatives

Mulching is a time and money saver as it reduces the amount of water and weeding your garden needs, but mulch itself can be expensive. That's why one of the best budget backyard ideas is to use an affordable mulch alternative.

Low-Cost Mulch Alternatives:

Grass Clippings: The next time you mow, rake up the clippings – and the savings – and spread them onto your flower beds.

Leaves: Shredded leaves make a great, cheap mulch alternative and provide nutrients to your plants.

Pine Needles: Pine needles are a relatively low-maintenance mulch alternative that is lightweight and easy to spread.

Compost: If you've already made your own compost bin, put it to good use in your landscaping. Just be careful not to layer it too thickly, as too much can heat up your plants and damage them.

Newspaper: After you're finished with the Sunday funny papers, let your plants take a peek layer about five pages on the ground, water lightly and then cover with topsoil before planting.

Stone: Stone mulch isn't right for all plants, but if used properly, it can cut down your weeding and maintenance costs in the long run. It's important to choose the right spot for your stone mulch: "Stone mulch works especially well in clean environments like around in-ground pool decks, traffic islands and narrow beds between buildings and pavement. This is because grass clippings and other organic matter won't be as likely to soil the stone mulch in such places. Also, stone mulch is less likely than wood mulch to wash onto pavements or blow into swimming pools."If your heart is set on traditional mulch, it's best to go with pine mulch,. "It's way cheaper than hardwood mulch and is easier to transport and spread."

2. Repurpose Old Tires

Tires are bulky and can be difficult to get rid of, as many waste haulers won't accept them. Why not put them to good use in your backyard? Recycled tires are inexpensive and easy to find. They can be picked up at a local recycling plant for a few dollars, but most people are willing to give away any old tires that they have on hand. Here are a few cheap landscaping ideas for your backyard using tires:

How to Landscape With Recycled Tires

Cover with outdoor pillow casings or rope for durable, rustic patio ottomans.

Stack and stagger tires to create decorative planters.

Create a hanging planter by filling one half with soil and attaching to a wall or fence.

Make a man-made garden pond using a tire as the base.

Give your kids a fun place to play with a recycled tire climber.

Vertical Garden with Red and Yellow Blooms

3. Go Vertical With Your Gardening

Love to garden but don't have a ton of space or money to do so? Consider a vertical garden.

Vertical gardening, simply put, is using vertical space to grow plants. If you're looking for small backyard landscaping ideas on a budget, vertical gardens are a good place to start. Not only do they make the most of limited space, but they can be inexpensive too, especially if you're using recycled materials like old plastic bottles to make it.

DIY Vertical Garden Ideas

Use a wooden ladder, terracotta pots and some wire for a rustic front porch vertical garden.

Wash out old paint cans, fill with soil and hang them up to create a vertical herb garden.

Repurpose a picture frame to create a vertical succulent garden.

Waterproof an unused shoe organizer for a vertical garden that's easy to move.

Turn your wooden fence into a vertical garden using a few pot hangers and wood screws.

4. Add a Splash of Color

Sometimes all it takes to make a backyard pop is to add some color. This can be as simple as painting planters to give your garden a more contemporary look, or giving wood, metal or plastic chairs a fresh coat of paint. To save even more on this budget backyard landscaping project, reuse leftover paint from previous projects instead of buying new paints.You can also add a ⊡uick splash of color in the form of flowers or foliage, positioning them on a deck, patio, at an entryway or tucked into a planting bed.

Pro Tip:

Another easy, affordable way to add natural tones to your backyard

is to give your deck a new coat of stain.

Learn how to maintain your deck to keep it beautiful year-round.

5. Plant Useful Plants

Cut grocery costs in the summer time by growing your own vegetables and herbs right in your own backyard. From DIY herb gardens to plants that repel bugs, you can easily turn your backyard into a space that's beautiful and functional with a few terracotta planters and the right placement. Cheap Natural Perennial Ground Covers for Landscaping on a Budget

6. Opt for Natural Perennial Ground Covers

Tired of weeding the lawn? Skip the weed killers and opt for dense spreading perennial ground covers instead. Weed killers can be both costly and hazardous to your health. "Harsh chemicals in Roundup can sicken pets and has been linked to cancer. Weed killers aren't just bad for your health they also pack a punch to your bank account at over $20 [per container]."

Pro Tip:

If your backyard is full of big, beautiful trees, you may want to choose shade plants that can handle living in their shadow, as not all plants can tolerate full or partial shade.

7. Build an Outdoor Fire Pit

There's no better way to bring the family together than with smores over a fire pit. But you don't need to spring for a contractor to put one in with one trip to the home improvement store, you can have your own backyard campfire station in just a few minutes. If you need to get rid of rocks from another project, building a fire pit with them is a great way to do it.

Here are a few affordable ideas to make your own DIY fire pit on a budget:

Fire Pit Ideas on a Budget

Concrete retaining wall blocks – about $1.25 per block, total cost of $50

Cinder block caps – about $1.50 per block, total cost of $40

Concrete fire bowl – about $3 for one bag of concrete, $56 total

Dirt floor fire ring – free, if using natural stones from your own woods

8. Plant a Tree

Planting trees is one of the easiest and least expensive backyard budget landscaping projects of all. All you need are a few digging tools, some mulch and the tree. Plus, having well-planned trees in your yard can end up saving you money in the long run. Planting shade trees is a common-sense solution that will save you money and make you more comfortable. Trees are simply a wise investment in future comfort and energy savings. Just take a minute and sit under one on a ninety-degree day and you'll understand this perfectly.

10. Use Affordable Lightning

Cheap outdoor string lights are a staple of budget backyard landscaping. Their soft, ambient glow can turn any patio into a chill summer hangout. White twinkle lights cost about $6 per strand, or for a more modern look, you can pick up a strand of clear globe lights for around $9. Though slightly more expensive, globe light strands are usually more durable than twinkle lights, and the bulbs are easily replaced. Once you've picked up affordable bulbs, try out these budget-friendly landscape   lighting   ideas:

Cheap Backyard Lighting Ideas

Wrap strands around outdoor pillars to create columns of light.

Run lights from house to tree using an eye bolt and an insulated cable to tie on a branch.

Create Texas lamp posts using wood posts, whiskey barrel planters and a little concrete.

Edge your flowerbeds with rope lights so you can see your hard-earned blooms even at night.

Drape your trees in lights for a charming, glowing backyard grove.

Rustic Outdoor Chairs Made of Wood, Sitting in a Grove of Perennial Ground Cover

10. Buy (or Build) Low-Cost Seating

Once you've finished your backyard budget landscaping projects, you'll want a place to sit back and enjoy the fruits of your labor. But no need to run to the furniture store you can easily search for used pieces online or make your own cheap outdoor seating right at home.

Cheap Outdoor Seating Ideas

Don't limit your searches to outdoor furniture; with a little waterproof sealant, you can turn regular indoor chairs or barstools into patio-worthy seating.

Not finding anything you like? Make your own cinder block and lumber bench.

Turn a tree stump into the perfect reading spot by attaching a waterproof cushion on top.

Use a leftover tire to create a durable seat with storage for kids.

Fix weatherproof cushions to milk crates for portable seating that can be easily stored.

When all else fails, drag a few old logs around your new fire pit for easy campfire seating.

Reuse and Recycle to Reduce Costs

The best backyard budget landscaping tip of all is to reuse and recycle items whenever possible. Visit your local thrift stores and check the classifieds online to find local garage sales. By purchasing used planters, furniture and even gardening tools to spruce up your lawn, you can save hundreds of dollars, and keep some really nice items out of the trash. Ultimately, to keep your backyard landscaping costs low, all you need is time and a little creativity.

Tips for Landscaping on a Budget
Save Money by Reducing Lawn Size

Many homeowners obsess over controlling lawn weeds. Their obsession drives them to spend money unnecessarily on weed killers such as crabgrass killers. If they are successful in these witch-hunts against weeds, the result may look good but produces an unhealthy monoculture.

The experts suggest accepting the presence of a certain number of weeds in the lawn. Their argument is that lawns with some diversity remain healthier than lawns reduced to a monoculture. While crabgrass may be unacceptable, there are some "good" weeds you should be willing to tolerate, such as wild violet (Viola sororia). These violets are not only pretty but also edible. Another beneficial weed is clover (Trifolium), which is a nitrogen-fixer, sharing this ability with other cover crops in the pea family. Clover will fertilize your lawn at no cost, thereby freeing you from adhering to a lawn-fertilizing schedule and saving you from spending money on chemical fertilizers.

Two questions may have popped into your mind at this point:

How do I go about reducing the size of my lawn? I do not wish to spray harsh chemicals on the grass to kill it because I want to be able to allow my children and/or pets to play in this area. After I reduce the size of my lawn, what do I put in place of the grass? Won't it cost just as much to maintain the area when something else is growing there? There are a number of ways to get rid of grass, including ways that stay away from chemical herbicide use. Perhaps the most popular method, currently, is laying down newspapers to kill the grass. What you replace the grass with largely comes down to your personal preferences and circumstances. Those with plain tastes who live in a rural setting and aren't interested in keeping up with the Joneses can simply lay down landscape fabric and cover it with the cheapest mulch they can find. Since the mulch won't be in direct contact with the soil, the process of decomposition will be slowed, yielding the money-saving result that you won't have to replace the mulch as often. If you want to dress up the area, there's no rule saying you cannot install a few container gardens there (as you would on a patio).

For those with more of a yen for plants, there are a number of possibilities, such as:

A mixed planting bed of perennials, ornamental grasses, and shrubs

Or more of a classic flower border

To stay on budget, make it a point to buy plants when they are on sale and/or from retailers known to sell them at a discount. Be aware, moreover, that some pretty ground covers will spread on their own and "fill in" an area. While that may sound bad to a gardener insistent on growing only well-behaved plants, such spreading might be just what you crave if you're looking to cover an area with plants without spending much money. Select drought-resistant plants to save money on watering. Once you have your plants in the ground, there are numerous money-saving ideas to follow in order to care for them while still staying within budget, including:

Watering plants early in the morning during the summer, rather than when temperatures heat up so that you lose less moisture to evaporation

Choosing easy-to-grow plants, so that you won't have to waste money on fertilizers or pesticides (or, in the worst-case scenario, replacing dead plants)

Tolerating the occasional hole that a bug chews in a leaf, rather than running out to buy an insecticide

Hardscape Needn't Break the Bank

Water features needn't bust the budget to make a big splash in your yard. Modern pumps and pond liners are inexpensive and easy for do-it-yourselfers to install. Add some stones and an extra bit of effort, and you can even build small waterfalls. Scrounge around for free stones at construction sites (obtain permission) or on the property of your country cousin. Or go slightly more upscale with a cascading clay pot fountain. Not only water features but other hardscape projects can be easier than beginners at first imagine. It's just a matter of choosing the path of least resistance. For instance, brick patios laid in sand are easier to build for do-it-yourselfers than those laid in concrete. By planning properly, it's also possible in many cases to avoid having to cut any of the bricks, a task daunting enough to drive many a homeowner into paying someone else to lay a patio for them. Similarly, bypass the pricey pros and lay your own stone walkways in sand.

Landscaping on a Budget With Cheap Plants

Obtaining cheap plants requires an adjustment in our attitudes. Many of us grew up buying plants from sources that specialize in the gardening trade. Such plants are high-quality, but that quality comes at a price. When shopping for cheap plants at sources that don't specialize in the gardening trade, we must resist the temptation to compare apples to oranges. For instance, cheap flowers at supermarkets will, in many cases, be of a quality inferior to that of the same plants found at your local nursery. But such plants will be less expensive, too, so the comparison is rather unfair. What you have to ask yourself is,

Do I have the time to sift through the cheap plants, in order to select acceptable specimens?

Do I have the time to give these cheap plants some extra TLC once I've planted them?

Is the extra time expended on selection and care justified by the money that I save?

If you answered these questions with a "Yes," then you're well on your way to success in landscaping on a budget. Purchasing cheap plants can result in a yard that looks like a million bucks but costs you relatively little. But there are two warnings about buying cheap plants: If you don't know what to look for to determine a plant's health, bring along someone who does. At the very least, inspect plants to see if they have any bugs or diseases on them. If they do, then they're not worth bringing home even if they're free. Once your cheap plants are in the ground, practice proper plant care. This is always sound advice, even for high-quality plants. But, in the case of cheap plants, a little extra TLC may be in order. For instance, if the plants have been stressed at the store, you may have to be extra-careful about watering them properly.

You can supplement your early shopping for annuals with the annuals that go on sale at nurseries in July and August. This is an inexpensive way to extend the time period during which your yard can be graced with colorful blooms. Also, some supermarkets put shrubs and perennials on sale at the end of the summer to avoid being stuck with inventory that they can't take care of during the winter.

Water Conservation Important in Saving Money

But landscaping on a budget goes beyond obtaining cheap plants. Some plants re🯀uire more water than others, and water is an increasingly precious commodity. Drought-tolerant perennials are better than most at fending for themselves, which lowers your water bill. Selecting drought-tolerant plants is one part of an overall water-conversation approach known as "xeriscaping . You can also save money on watering by installing automatic irrigation systems and by applying mulch. Container-gardening makes a lot of sense if space in your yard is limited. The idea makes even more sense if you can obtain cheap containers and plant them yourself. Inexpensive containers, including cemetery logs (which can serve as window boxes), can sometimes be purchased at yard sales. Just be careful to scour them out well in case they harbor any diseases. Whether planting in the ground or in containers, you'll need to fertilize your plants. But don't spend more than you need to on fertilizers when you can feed your plants for free. If you're serious about landscaping on a budget, then one of your first projects should be to build a compost bin. Then just place kitchen scraps, raked leaves, etc. into the compost bin, watering and mixing occasionally, and you'll have a ready source of soil amendments for free. If that sounds like too much work, some cities offer free compost at designated locations on a first-come-first-served basis. This compost is produced from vegetation removed by city work crews.

Low Maintenance Landscape Design Ideas for Backyard

Whereas a front yard is for the whole neighborhood to see, your backyard is about your own personal use. Here are some of our top low-maintenance backyard landscape design tips:

1. Add an Outdoor Rug

If you're looking to revitalize your patio space without making costly renovations, think about laying down a big outdoor rug. You can give your backyard a pop of color and transform your space without going to the trouble of staining or painting a deck.

2. Make a Trellis

Trellises are another great way to add some charm to your outdoor space. You can make your own using wooden boards or metal poles, and you can plant climbing roses on both sides.

3. Create a Pergola for Some Shade

If you like to spend a lot of time outside but don't always want the sun in your eyes, a pergola is a great solution. If you want extra shade, you can even add some curtains.

4. Buy a Fountain

If you have a small backyard and are looking for design ideas, buy a fountain! These items are an excellent way to add a water feature without spending too much or taking up too much space.

5. Add a Stock Tank Pool

A stock tank pool is an affordable way to cool down on those hot summer days and also it provides fun for your kids. Put it on a stone platform or concrete patio to avoid damaging your grass.

6. Add Some Mood Lighting

If you want the most beautiful backyard in the neighborhood, consider investing in some outdoor lighting. You can drape string lights on a pergola or across your outdoor space to create a starry-night feeling. Creating soft lighting by lining paths with lanterns and torches is another great idea.

7. Paint a Mural on Your Fence

Creating a distinctive mural on a fence is also an easy way to give your outdoor space an affordable makeover. To prepare your fence, just make sure to figure out which paints to use and decide on the scale or your masterpiece.

8. Try Xeriscaping

If you're interested in reducing your water usage, consider xeriscaping, which refers to planting drought-resistant plants in an arrangement that conserves water. It's easy, requires little maintenance and boosts the attractiveness of your yard and the value of your property.

9. Create an Outdoor Dining Space

If you love parties, barbecues or working outdoors, a table is indispensable to your outdoor space. You can make your own table using wooden boards and several wine barrels, or you can purchase a patio set with a table and chairs included.

10. Add Comfortable Seating

Don't forget to include comfy outdoor seating when transforming your outdoor space. Create a comfortable place for your family and guests to kick back with benches, rocking chairs and big outdoor pillows.

11. Stay Warm With a Fire Pit

Few items make for a memorable get-together like a fire pit. If you have some DIY experience, you can build your own using wall stones, or you can buy a metal one. Don't forget to add plenty of seating for when you roast marshmallows!

12. Add a Hammock

Hammocks are fun backyard fixtures for both children and adults. Suspend one between two sturdy trees and fasten its ropes using either tree straps or industrial hooks. If you have no sturdy trees in your yard, you can alternatively buy an affordable hammock with stands.

13. Create a Calming Space for Meditation

Pick a secluded place in your backyard, set up a table for incense and place some blankets and pillows for lounging. If this spot happens to be close to a tree, you can also hang chairs or some decorative ornaments to give your space more flair.

14. Set Up a Theater

Enjoy all your favorite films right from the comfort of your backyard by hooking up a screen and projector, laying down some blankets and pillows and hanging up some string lights.

15. Create a Fun Zone for Kids

If you have little ones running around, a jungle gym, swing set, treehouse or a tire swing is a backyard necessity.

Easy Front Yard Landscaping Ideas

Whereas your backyard is dedicated to fun for you, your friends and your family, your front yard is what you show off to neighbors and passers-by. A well-designed, well-maintained front yard will create a great first impression for all who enter your home including potential buyers. Here are a few simple ways to make this important outdoor space stand out:

1. A Post and Rail Fence

While you may associate fences with keeping out prying eyes, post and rail fences are meant to attract passers-by. They do so by defining the borders of your property. Generally speaking, a defined area whether it be defined by fences, hedges or stone walls is more attractive than an open-ended space.

2. Driveway Design

If you've defined your front yard with a fence, hedge or wall, chances are it is breached by your driveway. At the entrance to the driveway, you can choose to frame it with a driveway gate. Make sure to keep the landscaping around your driveway's entrance well maintained, as this area greatly impacts a passer-by's first impression of the property.

Principles of landscape design

There are six principles of design that have been used by artists for centuries throughout all art forms, painting and floral design as well as landscape design. They are:

Balance

Focalization

Simplicity

Rhythm and Line

Proportion

Unity

1. Balance

Balance is a state of being as well as seeing. We are most comfortable in landscapes that have a sense of balance. There are two major types of balance: symmetrical and asymmetrical. Symmetrical balance is used in formal landscapes when one side of the landscape is a mirror image ofthe opposite side. These landscapes often use geometric patterns in the walkways, planting beds and even how the plants are pruned into shapes. This type of balance appears to be rather stiff in appearance and often is highly maintained. Asymmetrical balance, also known as informal balance, differs from one side to the other and appears to be relaxing and free flowing. Using these principles, landscape designers create landscapes that are pleasing to look at and even inviting. These principles were not created by artists centuries ago, but more of an inherent visual sense that most people possess. Using these as guidelines helps designers and homeowners create a landscape that "make sense" to look at.

2. Focalization

Any good design has a focal point the place where the viewer's eye is first attracted. Focalization is sometimes referred to as focalization of interest or simply focal point. The focal point is the strongest element in the design in any given view. A home's focal point is often the front door. The landscape focal point is often something close to the front door to enhance the entrance of the home. Each area of the landscape may include a focal point, but it is certainly not necessary. Landscape designers should not overuse focal points. In any view, people are attracted to interesting plant forms, bright colors and artistic, architectural design as well as art or sculptures. Mix it up, have some fun and create interesting focal points.

3. Simplicity

Simplicity is what the name implies simple. Keeping landscapes simple, not cluttered or fussy is always a good practice. This is not the opposite of complexity. Many landscapes have very complex features, including the architectural design, water features and extensive lighting features.

Landscapes that makepeople happy and comfortable avoid using too many colors, shapes, curves and textures, but in no way does this mean simplistic, boring or lack of imagination.

4. Rhythm and line

When something in the landscape is repeated with a standard interval, a rhythm is established. In landscape design, the interval is usually space. Plants, groups of plants, lamp posts, benches or other structures can be repeated within the design to create this rhythm. Lines within a landscape are created in a landscape by the shape and form of the planting beds, sidewalks, where the turf meets pavement and other hardscaping features. The rhythm and line design principle gives a landscape a sense of movement and is what may draw you "into" the landscape. This is what makes landscapes calming to our souls.

5. Proportion

Proportion refers to the size relationship of all the features in the landscape. This includes vertical, horizontal and special relationships. Short people, tall people and children all perceive space differently. Proportion in landscape design extends to building size, lot size, plant size, areas of plantings to areas of open space as well as the use of the landscape.

6. Unity

The principle of unity is easily measured if the other five landscape principles have been properly executed throughout the landscape. Unity in design simply means all the separate parts of the landscape work together to create a great total design. Colors, shapes, sizes, textures and other features work together to create a unified space. Patterns and colors are often repeated. Lighting, special features, bed shapes and hardscapes such as walk ways all need to work together to create a pleasing look and a unified landscape.

CONCLUSION

Armed with a realistic and well-thought-out landscaping plan, you can spread out the work and expense over several years. Take it one step at a time to keep your project from becoming overwhelming. Remember, this is supposed to be fun! You are creating a space for you to enjoy. Small steady improvements over the years can transform your yard into the paradise you envision.

Printed in Great Britain
by Amazon

70575925R00023